MW00989899

Virtue Victorious over Vice. Sketch by Parmigianino (Girolamo Francesco Maria Mazzola), Florence, Italy, c. 1520.

Bloomsbury USA

An imprint of Bloomsbury Publishing Plc

1385 Broadway
New York
NY 10018
USA

50 Bedford Square
London
WC1B 3DP
UK

www.bloomsbury.com

First U.S. edition 2018

ISBN: HB: 978-1-63557-083-0

Library of Congress Cataloging-in-Publication Data is available.

2 4 6 8 10 9 7 5 3 1

Designed and typeset by Wooden Books Ltd, Glastonbury, UK

Printed in the U.S.A. by Worzalla, Stevens Point, Wisconsin

To find out more about our authors and books visit
www.bloomsbury.com. Here you will find extracts, author interviews,
details of forthcoming events, and the option to sign up for our newsletters.

Bloomsbury books may be purchased for business or promotional use.
For information on bulk purchases please contact Macmillan Corporate and
Premium Sales Department at specialmarkets@macmillan.com.

ETHICS

THE ART OF CHARACTER

Gregory R. Beabout

with additional content by Mike Hannis

BLOOMSBURY
NEW YORK · LONDON · OXFORD · NEW DELHI · SYDNEY

To my parents

With special thanks to Cindy and my family, and to good friends who are good characters: Chuck, George, and Michael. Also, thanks to John Martineau for his patient persistence and creativity with editing and layout, and to Mike Hannis for his teamwork and incisive contributions in writing. Thanks, finally, to the Warburg Institute, London, for access to their picture library. Cartoons are from Cartoonstock.

Recommended classic texts: Plato, Republic; *Aristotle,* Nicomachean Ethics; *Augustine,* City of God, Book XIX; *Thomas Aquinas,* Summa Theologiae; *John Stuart Mill,* Utilitarianism; *Kant,* Groundwork of the Metaphysics of Morals; *Alasdair MacIntyre,* After Virtue; *Julia Annas,* Intelligent Virtue. *For a good collection, see Gordon Marino,* Ethics: The Essential Writings. *For thoughtful approaches to applied ethics, see Alejo Sison,* Happiness and Virtue Ethics in Business; *Edmund Pellegrino,* The Virtues in Medical Practice; *Patrick Curry,* Ecological Ethics *(2nd ed.).*

Above, and front cover: Temperance, surrounded by the seven liberal arts; clockwise from lower left: Arithmetic, Music, Rhetoric, Astronomy, Geometry, Logic, and Grammar. Engraved by Philips Galle [1537–1612] from an original drawing by Pieter Bruegel the Elder [1525–1569], Netherlands.

CONTENTS

Above: Virtue, proceeded by Folly and followed by Glory. Engraving by Giulio Bonasone [1498–1580], Bologna, Italy. Courtesy of the Warburg Institute, London.

INTRODUCTION

You can't learn ethics from a book. To learn honesty, one must practice telling the truth. To learn justice, one must act in a just manner. The same is true of generosity, courage, kindness, patience, and all the virtues. This applies to any worthwhile complicated human endeavor. To learn to play the piano, you have to play the piano. To learn to play basketball, you need actual experience with a ball and a hoop. To learn to drive an automobile you'll need to get behind the wheel.

So, in cases where learning comes with practice, why *are* there instruction books? Besides, isn't ethics fundamentally different from skill acquisition? One can be masterfully accomplished at basketball or driving without being ethical. A trained physician has the skill to heal or to wound, and those who are artful in grammar, logic, and rhetoric can inspire or manipulate. Skill at using words, whether on the page, in one's mind, or in speech, seems entirely separate from ethics.

Or is it? Those who develop technical mastery in any domain eventually are faced with questions of deep purpose. How should one's skills be used? What goals are worth pursuing?

The ancient Greeks used the term *ethike* in debating how to live a good and worthwhile life. Tracing their arguments about the art of character and learning the history of moral philosophy won't make you ethical. Certainly reading this little book on the good life won't make you richer or thinner or sexier. However, it just might help you on your journey to approach the authentic and ancient task of ethics: to craft a beautiful life.

WHAT IS ETHICS?
like this, not that

Ethics is an ancient term with a Greek pedigree. The philosopher Aristotle [384–322 BC] noted that, in Greek, *ethike* has meanings that are complex and ambiguous. Two Greek letters—*eta* and *epsilon*—are similar to the English letter *e* (*eta* has a faintly longer *ê*-sound than *epsilon*), and the Greek words *ethike* and *ethos* can be pronounced or spelled with either Greek *e*, slightly altering the meaning.

Spelled one way, *ethos* refers to the farm building where animals are kept. For example, in Homer's *Iliad*, the word *ethos* is used to designate the horse stable. Horses that run away tend to return (eventually) to this secure, stable location. Spelled the other way, *ethos* is a character trait, a personal quality that is reliable and persistent. In unusual circumstances, one may act out of character, but generally, *ethos* is stable, both in an individual life and in a community.

An excellent character trait (*ethike arête*) is an acquired personal quality that an excellent person "has." The Romans, seeking to translate into Latin the idea of a trait one has, called it a *habitus*. The excellent person "has it." In English, the meaning devolved; we tend to think that a habit is rote, routine, and perhaps sub-rational. That's not what the ancients meant at all. To be ethical is to have formed one's life in such a way that, through deliberate excellent actions, one has confirmed and consolidated those qualities of character and intellect that make for a worthwhile and beautiful human existence.

In conversation with Socrates, the military general Laches expressed the ambivalence we often feel about "ethics talk." As Laches put it:

2

When I hear someone discussing virtue and wisdom, especially a true man worthy of the topic, I am delighted beyond measure . . . but when a man's words and actions do not agree, it annoys me. – [88d-e]

Kant once quipped that two things provoke the most wonder and awe: the starry sky above and the moral law within. Humans have long huddled around the warm glow of a shared fire to trade tales of trial and truth that shed light on the eternal questions: Where are we going? Why? What makes for a good life? How does a human live well?

Many ancient stories contain sage advice about survival and human relations. They involve familiar stock characters: the mighty hero, the beautiful but boasting mother, the weak king, inseparable brothers, a jealous wife, the kind gentle shepherd, the rash fighter, and so forth. We meet a similar cast of characters in star-lore, fables, fairy tales, and folksongs. These provide a sort of field guide for social life. "Be aware of this one; be like that one; not like that one."

At its ancient core, ethics is not primarily about words or theories or knowledge or rules. It is the art of character. Reflection on the art of character and the requirements of conscience begins with and draws from the characters we've met during evening story time, and with the wonder that comes from gazing at the heavens.

after Arthur Rackham [1867-1939]

3

CHARACTER AND CODES
virtues or rules?

Many ancient vows, such as the Hippocratic Oath (*see page 49*), involve a pledge to live according to a "*set of traits*." In contrast, contemporary "codes of ethics" tend to focus on specific *actions*, rather than considering a person's whole life and character. Modern codes are almost always framed as a "*set of rules*."

The terms "ethics" and "morality" have a complicated history. *Ethos* and *ethike* in Greek refer to character, not rules; Cicero translated these into Latin as *moralis*. Until the Renaissance, studies of ethics or morality focused on character formation and development, but during the European Enlightenment, philosophers began to narrow the moral debate to actions, aiming to discover the rational basis for determining right action, later focusing on either utility or duty (*see pp. 43–45*).

In the early 20th century, academic debates about *normative ethics* (discussion of which acts or action-types are right or wrong) gave way to discussions of *meta-ethics* (theoretical questions about the meaning of moral terms, the nature of moral judgments, and whether these are rationally defensible).

Of course, the ancient world had rules too. *The Code of Hammurabi* had 282 laws, including many that now seem problematic, such as "an eye for an eye, a tooth for a tooth." Certain passages resemble the

B.de

"Are you capable of distinguishing right from wrong?"

"Can you give me a *hint?*"

4

Mosaic Law and rules advanced by the Hittites, Assyrians, and others. Such lists prohibit and prescribe actions regarding trade, theft, killing, slander, the distribution of food, the duties of workers, and so on.

"WHEN'S HAPPY HOUR?"

Problems arise when ethics is conceived only in terms of rules. Life is complex, so no set of rules can be specific enough to cover every circumstance. A rule-based approach tends to encourage searching for loopholes and "gaming the system." Rules can conflict, and often require interpretation. If ethics is nothing but rules, then further rules will be needed to decide what to do when rules and interpretations conflict. Such problems show why it can be seen as better to understand ethics as having to do, first and foremost, with character. Actions shape character, including the action of following good rules.

> The law prescribes that the works of a courageous person be done (for example, that a soldier not break rank or flee), as well as those of a temperate person (for example, not committing adultery or wanton aggression) and those of a gentle person (for example, not striking people or verbally abusing them). Well-formed laws prescribe some things and forbid others. – Aristotle [1129b19-21]

Ethics consists in learning to live well. It is a quest to develop and excel in the traits needed to flourish, obeying good rules while acquiring the wisdom to distinguish between good and bad ones.

SOCRATES
stinging criticism

When he was young, Socrates [470–399 BC] studied the natural world, puzzling to understand the earth and the heavens. As he matured, his focus shifted. The logical methods of rational argumentation he learned from the "nature philosophers" were redirected to an inquiry about how to live an excellent human life.

Plato recounts that this change occurred after Socrates's impetuous friend Chaerephon asked the Pythian prophetess whether anyone was wiser than Socrates. Challenged by the answer that there is "none wiser," Socrates set off to seek someone wiser, meeting rhetoricians, politicians, and writers. Finding many of these fellow citizens full of fakery, he persisted in asking awkward questions (describing himself as a gadfly), unmasking those who claimed to know what they did not.

He among you is the wisest who knows that his wisdom is really worth nothing at all. – Socrates, attrib. by Plato [*Apology* 23b]

His stinging attacks were a nuisance, so charges were brought against him. At his trial, he defended himself by comparing the city of Athens to a great racehorse that had become sluggish until stung awake by his questioning. He exhorted his fellow citizens to share his quest for virtue, and by seeking to practice the virtues, to stir up a better life.

Socrates discovered only what is available to every reflective adult: the quest for authentic self-understanding involves acknowledging one's limitations. He engaged in dialogue as part of a life of honest self-examination, in order to better himself and his community. To

Above: Socrates, found guilty of impiety and corrupting the youth of Athens, follows his rule of obedience to the law and carries out his own execution by drinking hemlock.

fix your eyes on the stars takes focus, but it is harder to gaze intently into your soul. Most of us blink and look away.

The poet, politician, and rhetorician who brought charges against Socrates perhaps worried that their questions and criticisms would destabilize the social institutions crucial to their power and prestige. The three accusers were part of the new class of "knowledge workers" in the golden age of Greece, master wordsmiths who claimed expertise in a skill advertised as crucial for success. Socrates suspected them of caring more about wealth and power than character, conscience, and the common good.

The unexamined life is not worth living. – Socrates, attrib. by Plato [*Apology 37e*]

Understanding Socrates is not difficult. Living like Socrates is.

PLATO'S CAVE
shadow and light

Socrates left no written works, but his followers took on the task of *paideia*, the moral and cultural education of Greek citizens preparing for good leadership. One such follower, Isocrates [436–338 BC], is sometimes called the father of liberal education, because his school emphasized grammar, dialectical reasoning, and rhetoric as disciplines needed to excel in speech and to shape virtuous souls. Isocrates taught that good speaking (*eu legein*) is allied to good prudential action (*eu prattein*), and hoped that his fine written speeches might promote civic education.

The crosstown rival to the school of Isocrates was the Academy, founded by Plato [428–348 BC]. We have no textbooks from Plato's curriculum. Instead, we have dialogues, including Plato's masterful classic, the *Republic*, in which Socrates is depicted engaging in a wide-ranging conversation that includes a plan for educating a just soul. In one of the most famous sections, the "Allegory of the Cave," Socrates presents what he calls a "parable of the soul's education."

> *Imagine humans dwelling in a cave from childhood, fettered, only able to look in one direction at images on a wall.* – Plato [514a]

One prisoner is released. He turns to see a track of puppets, and behind it a fire. Realizing he has been staring at shadows, he ascends for the first time out of the cave, where he is overcome by the light of the upper world. Looking down, he notices shadows on the ground. As his eyes adjust, he is able to gaze upward, observing actual plants and animals, then the moon and stars, until finally he glimpses the

Above: Plato's Cave. A lantern casts shadows of puppets on to a wall. Prisoners, living in the dark, see only the shadows on the wall, and mistake them for real things. Philosophers, meanwhile, stand beneath the lantern, considering the idea that they too may be but shadows, cast by a greater light.

overwhelming brilliant illumination of the sun. Recognizing that his life in the cave had been a shadowy imprisonment in illusions, he feels compelled to return to enlighten his friends below of the dazzling upper world. This, of course, does not go well.

The art of guiding a soul toward the highest good, according to Plato, involves creating the conditions for a transformation of perspective, from the shadowy world of appearances (in which one is attracted to the shifting allure of wealth, pleasure, and power) to an increasingly deeper, more penetrating, enlightened vision of that "ever fixed mark," the highest good.

> *The journey upwards is the ascent of the soul. The last thing to be seen, and hardly seen, is the idea of the good.* – Plato [517b]

NICOMACHEAN ETHICS
crafting character

The most important ethics text ever published isn't really a book. Aristotle's *Nicomachean Ethics* [dated around 330 BC] has been studied for millennia, but there is no reliable account of the development of its contents. Almost certainly, the text is based on lecture notes modified throughout Aristotle's career. If so, it is, as Alasdair MacIntyre observed, "the most brilliant set of lecture notes ever written."

Several ancient sources suggest that "Nicomachus" was the name of Aristotle's son, to whom the text may have been dedicated. Perhaps he played an editorial role, transforming the lectures into book form.

Aristotle says the lectures are "not suited for a young man." Instead, he addresses himself to a person experienced in life, a listener poised to take a leadership role in the life of a community. Such a person was likely well brought up, with a desire to pursue the common good and in possession of a sense of what it is to live a beautiful, meaningful life. It is not a book intended for ethical theorists.

> *The present inquiry does not aim at theoretical knowledge, for we are inquiring not to know what goodness is, but to become good.* – Aristotle [1103b27]

For twenty years Aristotle was a student and then a young teacher at Plato's Academy, where he focused on rhetoric. After Plato died, Aristotle left Athens to spend several years doing biological field studies in the Greek islands, collecting and categorizing specimens of plants and animals. Against that background, the *Nicomachean Ethics* can be read as a "field guide" to human character, and this in two senses:

First and foremost, Aristotle aims to build up in his listener those qualities of character and intellect needed to flourish as a member of the human species. As Aristotle observed, the human being is a *zōon politikon*, a speaking animal whose powers of life are actualized not by mere instinct, but in a community through the development of language and the realization of rational powers of deliberation, judgment, and responsible action. Accordingly, the hero of Aristotle's story is the person of practical wisdom.

Secondly, the *Nicomachean Ethics* contains a familiar cast of characters: the boaster, the ironist, the boor, the buffoon, the coward, the rash man, the generous bountiful person, the glutton, the fool, the gentle one, the hothead, the unjust, the shameless, and many others. Joining the conversation with Aristotle, we are invited to reflect upon which traits of character to purge from our habits, and which are integral to a beautiful life worth crafting.

Above: A procession of Shakespearean characters, representing a range of character traits.
Which of these traits should we keep, and which should we purge? London, 1769.

Becoming Responsible
preconditions of virtue

In the *Nicomachean Ethics*, Aristotle presumes a listener who is a decent person of judgment with a well-rounded background, one who is able to discern which kind of knowledge is suitable for the context at hand.

> It is the mark of an educated person to look for precision in each class of things just so far as the nature of the subject admits; it is evidently equally foolish to accept probable reasoning from a mathematician and to demand from a rhetorician scientific proofs. – Aristotle [1094b25]

The subject of ethics presupposes an engaged participant who is responsible for their actions, the formation of their character, and their life. Our actions are up to us, at least some of the time, and to some extent; and although each of us is given specific tendencies as part of our biology and upbringing, our character development depends in part on our voluntary actions and deliberate decisions.

We tend to praise and blame people for their voluntary actions, while feeling sympathy and pity for counter-voluntary ones, which may result from force or lack of knowledge. Force can be either physical: "I trod on your toe because the wind blew me," or psychological: "Threatened by violence, I acted strangely." Lack of knowledge can involve either ignorance of relevant particularities: "I didn't know it was your apple I ate," or relevant principles: "No one ever told me it's wrong to eat other people's apples." Negligence, of particularities or principles, is excusable only when it is not voluntary, and culpable when it comes from lack of due care.

Decisions craft character. Each decision a person makes is a voluntary, all-things-considered judgment of what to do here and now, something practical to which they are committed. In cases where the outcome is undetermined, unclear, or uncertain, deliberation is required, involving attention to relevant particularities, multiple perspectives, and pertinent principles and purposes.

Living an unhealthy life will lead to physical deterioration, and in the same way a character can become "sick" by doing actions that are greedy, self-centered, or thoughtless. We are each responsible for our actions and (with some qualifications) our character states. Acting depends on us, and so does not acting. By each decision, by each yes or no, we are ourselves responsible, to some extent, for who we become.

Above: Castle of Virtue, Italian, 16th C. Virtues need to be developed and protected.

13

HAPPINESS
and the good life

What makes for a good life? The poor may imagine it is money; the ill, health. In modern consumer cultures, happiness has become tied to getting whatever you want whenever you want it, so is viewed as a psychological state which "happens" when preferences are satisfied.

> *People seem to get their suppositions about happiness and the good life from their own lives.* – Aristotle [1095b15]

For the classical philosophers, the question "What is *eudaimonia*?"— or the Latin equivalent, "What is *beatitudo*?"—was a matter of prime importance. Rather than moment-to-moment experiences "happening" and bringing short-term pleasure, happiness is about the entire narrative of a life, unfolding through multiple chapters.

> *The ultimate end of human acts is eudaimonia, happiness in the sense of living well.* – Hannah Arendt

Considered this way, happiness has the quality of a goal, desirable in itself rather than for the sake of something else. Human purposes are often nested within deeper goals, and even when not quite aware of the motive, humans often act to aim at a target. Aristotle suggests that our ultimate target is not a quantifiable product like a trophy for the winner, but a quality of self-actualization in a complete life.

> *He is happy who lives in accordance with complete virtue and is sufficiently equipped with external goods, not for some chance period, but throughout a complete life.* – Aristotle [1101a10]

Accordingly, happiness is not preference-satisfaction; *eudaimonia* is a life of flourishing or well-being fitted to humanity, and especially to what is best in people. This raises a series of questions:

- *What qualities of character constitute a happy life?*
- *What dispositions count as virtues, not only in a social role, but in a human life?*
- *How is virtue distinguished from vice?*

Puzzling through these questions follows upon an understanding of happiness as well-being, and brings us closer to our ultimate goal:

Since happiness is an activity of soul in accordance with complete virtue, we must consider the nature of virtue, for perhaps this will help us see better the nature of happiness. – Aristotle [1102a1]

Above: Happiness, as a wedding feast, Wenceslas Hollar [1607–77], after Pieter Bruegel the Elder.

TWO KINDS OF GOALS
performance and results

Aristotle begins the *Nicomachean Ethics* by drawing an important distinction between two kinds of goals.

Some are activities. Others are products apart from the activities. – [1094a3]

INSTRUMENTAL ACTIVITY aims at a specific end product: a carpenter builds in order to produce a house, and a painter's brushstrokes are directed toward a completed painting.

AUTOTELIC ACTIVITY, by contrast, is pursued for its own sake, often with a sense of internal purpose: the goal of the dancer is to dance. Autotelic activities include those pursued in the spirit of play, such as games which ignite energy and personal passion.

Play is a uniquely adaptive act, not subordinate to some other adaptive act, but with a special function of its own in human experience. – Huizinga, Homo Ludens

The mystique of rock climbing is climbing; you get to the top of a rock glad it's over but really wish it would go on forever. The justification of climbing is climbing, like the justification of poetry is writing . . . – Csikszentmihalyi, Flow

The two goals are well illustrated in Alasdair MacIntyre's story of a child, initally incited to learn the game of chess by bribes of candy, who finally becomes motivated instead by internal goals of analytical skill, strategic imagination, and competitive intensity. The mastery of any social practice involves a shift from mere results-oriented given-ends (where moral shortcuts can seem attractive), to a passion for performance-oriented guiding-ends. Research suggests that this shift strengthens integrity of character. Psychologist Martin Seligman identifies five elements crucial for human well-being:

> P *is positive emotion,* E *is engagement,* R *is relationships,* M *is meaning and* A *is accomplishment. Those are the five elements of what free people choose to do. Pretty much everything else is in service of one or more of these goals.*
>
> — Martin Seligman, *Flourish*

Building on this, Mihaly Csikszentmihalyi (*quoted opposite*) describes optimal human experience in a similar manner to Aristotle's description of *eudaimonia*: a musician who loses herself in her music, an athlete who is completely present in the experience of intense competition, or a scientist immersed in the investigation of a complex problem. In each case skills and challenges tend to be higher than average. The Taoist scholar Chuang Tzu described this as "walking without touching the ground" or "flowing," while the Stoics described the goal of human happiness as *eurhoia biou*: a smooth flow of life.

Left: Chinese philosopher Chuang Tzu, 4th century BC. Chuang Tzu and Hui Shi were walking beside a waterfall when Chuang Tzu said, "See how the minnows come out and dart around where they please! That's what fish really love!" Hui Shi said, "You're not a fish—how do you know what fish enjoy?" Chuang Tzu said "I know it by standing here beside the river."

EXCELLENCE OF CHARACTER
cultivating virtue

Good character, like the acquisition of a skill, is developed through repeated deliberate decisions. Although some people are gifted with good looks, health, a good upbringing, and so forth, none of these fortunes guarantee good character—even the gifted can make a mess of their lives.

So what is excellence of character (Greek: *arête*; Latin: *virtus*)? Is it a feeling? Not quite. While some virtues refine feelings, there is a difference, since feelings can come and go, but excellence of character, once established through deliberate decisions, becomes relatively fixed as a stable trait. Is virtue a capacity? Not really. A child who is naturally outgoing has the capacity to grow up friendly, or perhaps annoying. In that way, the capacity of a child might be described as a sort of "first nature," while good character, once formed, becomes "second nature."

The virtues are acquired first by imitating those more excellent than oneself. By deliberately repeating and perfecting the good actions of an exemplary model, excellence of character is confirmed and consolidated in one's choices. We become what we repeatedly do.

> Those things we have to learn before we can do them we learn by doing: humans become carpenters by building houses, and harpists by playing the harp. We become just by practicing just actions, self-controlled by exercising self-control, and courageous by performing acts of courage. – Aristotle [1103a32]

A virtue is a disposition, an acquired personal quality that persists across time in various contexts. While Homer and the epic storytellers spoke frequently of physical virtues (the strength of Odysseus, the beauty of Helen), the excellences praised by ethicists are qualities of character. These excellences involve a "balanced harmony" between too much and too little. As with physical exercise, where excess and deficiency can each harm, finding the "golden mean" is context-sensitive with variations relative to the person(s) involved:

> *Virtue is the sort of disposition that is concerned with choice, lying in a mean of the sort relative to the context, determined by a rational principle, and by that principle by which a person of practical wisdom would determine it.* – [1107a1]

So, for example, generosity is a virtue whereby a person is disposed to open-handedly offer money, time, or help to others without either acting like a miserly penny-pincher, or being wastefully extravagant.

Aristotle's lecture notes refer to a "chart" of virtuous traits, which scholars have been able to recreate from his discussion (*see too page 58*):

ACTION/FEELING	DEFICIENCY	MEAN	EXCESS
FEAR AND DARING	*cowardice*	*courage*	*rashness*
PLEASURES OF TOUCH/TASTE	*insensibility*	*temperance*	*self-indulgence*
GIVING AND RECEIVING	*stinginess*	*generosity*	*extravagance*
SELF-PRESENTATION	*smallness*	*magnanimity*	*vanity*
ANGER	*lack of spirit*	*gentleness*	*crankiness*
SELF-EXPRESSION	*mock modesty*	*truthfulness*	*boastfulness*
CONVERSATION	*boorishness*	*wit*	*buffoonery*
SOCIAL CONDUCT	*cantankerousness*	*friendliness*	*obsequiousness*

THE CARDINAL VIRTUES
excellent hinges

The phrase "cardinal virtues" originates with Ambrose [340–397], bishop of Milan. Famous for his rhetorical eloquence, Ambrose delivered one of his greatest orations at the funeral of his brother. In the speech he identifies four excellent traits in his sibling, which he calls "*cardo*," Latin for "hinge." The name stuck, since these traits open the door to a good life, and excellence of character turns on them.

In art, common props and symbols traditionally identify these four excellences (*see opposite*). *Courage* is often shown wearing armor and escorting a lion as a sign of brave strength. *Moderation* pours the proper balance of water and wine between two jugs. *Justice* holds fair and balanced scales and a sword that protects and enforces righteousness. *Wisdom* or prudence gazes into a mirror of self-knowledge to approach the truth in its full complexity by recognizing multiple perspectives.

All other virtues can be said to hinge on these four excellent human traits. The three theological virtues (*faith*, *hope*, and *charity*) flower from the four cardinal virtues, while other virtues are corollaries. For example, patience takes courage (to withstand difficulties in others); gratitude flows from justice (to recognize and respond to gifts granted).

HUMAN POWER	CARDINAL VIRTUE	GREEK	LATIN
fight/flight response	COURAGE	*andreia*	*fortitudo*
desire for touch and taste	MODERATION	*sôphrosunê*	*temperantia*
intelligence	WISDOM	*phronesis*	*prudentia*
social relations	JUSTICE	*dikaiosunê*	*iustitia*

Ambrose's fourfold structure also appears in more ancient texts:

> Conduct oneself with courage in danger; moderation in foregoing pleasures; wisdom in choosing between good and evil; justice in giving each what is due.
>
> — Cicero, De Officiis [I, ii, 5]

> Wisdom is the leader: next follows moderation; and from the union of these two with courage springs justice. — Plato, Laws [631c]

In *The Republic* (IV), Socrates privileges these same four *arête*, assuming a wide acceptance of them as the core qualities in an excellent human. These virtues perfect four fundamental powers of life in the human soul and the well-formed community. Moderation tempers and completes appetites. Courage brings order and excellence to the spirit. Justice is ordered balance within the soul and in relation to others. Wisdom or prudence is excellence in thought-guiding action.

Cicero giving his book to his son Marcus. Frontispiece to Cicero, De Officiis, Venice, 1525.

COURAGE
fight or flight

When animals sense a threat, they become alert and ready. Similarly, when faced by danger, humans will either run away, freeze, hold ground, or attack. Human reflective power adds a layer of complexity. Rather than just reacting to circumstance, the virtuous person is self-possessed and in command of their primal responses. Some dangers are sudden and obvious, while others, such as illness, poverty, and abandonment, lurk and creep. Courage involves appropriating one's impulses and responding to each situation with the proper balance of apprehension and confidence. Too much courage can lead to rash behavior; too little, to cowardice. The courageous person has fortitude in the face of difficulties, including the practice of virtue itself.

Without courage, you can't practice any other virtue consistently. – Maya Angelou

Women fighting Devils, Florence, 1460.

Moderation
temperance

We all get hungry—whether for food, possessions, excitement, attention, or power. However, developing a taste for the right things in the right way, in the right amounts, at the right times, for the right reasons is not easy. Consumer culture says that "greed is good" and "bigger is better," but this is a recipe for slavery, not liberation. Unbridled acquisitiveness becomes *pleonexia*, the insatiable and ruthless desire to acquire more and more, an infinite appetite for finite things. Unchecked ambition results in prideful *hubris*. As Epictetus [55–135 AD] noted:

If one oversteps the bounds of moderation, the greatest pleasures cease to please.

To practice *sôphrosunê* (moderation) is to embody calm self-mastery:

Self-knowledge is the very essence of moderation, and in this I agree with him who dedicated the inscription 'Know thyself' at Delphi. – Plato, *Charmides* [164d]

The first steps toward self-possession usually involve restraint, learning to recognize which inclinations need to be tempered, to achieve a balanced mean between self-indulgence (too little moderation) and self-denial (too much). As the saying goes, all things in moderation—even moderation itself (*see too the illustration opposite the contents, p. iv*).

When a man is stimulated by his own thoughts, full of desire and dwelling on what is attractive, his craving increases even more. He is making the fetter even stronger. But he who takes pleasure in stilling his thoughts, practising the contemplation of what is repulsive, and remaining recollected, now he will make an end of craving, he will snap the bonds... – Buddha [563–483 BC]

JUSTICE
in the house

Humans are highly social animals, and our power to communicate (perfected in artful grammar, logic, and rhetoric) points to our need to cultivate a disposition that improves social relationships. Justice is the virtue that disposes one to give others their due.

> *Rational speech (logos) is for making clear what is beneficial or harmful, and hence also what is just or unjust. For it is special to human beings, in comparison to other animals, that they alone have perception of what is just or unjust.* – Aristotle [1253a15]

The character of "Lady Justice" (*see opposite*) dates back millennia. In ancient Egypt, as *Ma'at*, she held a scale to measure the weight of each human soul against the "feather of truth." Later, Roman artists portrayed *Iustitia* by combining features of two Greek goddesses: *Themis* (who orders the seasons) and *Dike* (who balances custom and law). Although women in the ancient world could not vote or appear in court, Justice was nevertheless imagined as a fair and balanced woman.

By the early modern period she had gained a blindfold to portray (visual) impartiality, and a double-edged sword for truth, reason, and certain punishment. Lady Justice reminds the crowd that they can outnumber and eventually defeat any strong individual or group. The logic of *might makes right* gives way to the logic of custom, and eventually to a principle of defending and enforcing fairness and equality.

A deeper understanding of justice points beyond social conventions to more universal principles: equality, even-handedness, and shared liberty. Indeed, puzzles about how to treat equal cases equally have a long tradition, from Plato's *Republic* to *A Theory of Justice* by John Rawls [1921–2002], and beyond.

From a public perspective, justice is the decisive criterion for moral action in social relations, whereas from a subjective perspective, justice is complete virtue exercised in relation to others. Thus, the justice of one's character is revealed by the way one treats others when in a position of power or leadership, whether at home, at work, or abroad.

Justice and its meaning are central to debates about ethics, including vast bodies of literature that take up questions about the equitable exchange of goods and the fulfillment of contractual obligations (*commutative* justice), the allocation of economic benefits and burdens (*distributive* justice), the appropriate punishment for criminals and victims (*restorative* justice), and the best type of institutions for cultivating balanced order in society (*political* justice).

Justice, blindfolded, holding scales and a sword; by Pieter Bruegel the Elder [1525–1569].

WISDOM
dear prudence

The most important of the cardinal virtues is *phronesis*, or practical wisdom. *Phronesis* is the habit of knowing the right action, at the right time, in the right way, for the right reason. A person who embodies this trait (the *phronimos*) has mastered the ability to see, judge, and act.

This virtue, of which some commentators have said that there is no real vice of excess, must at first be taught, but is then later developed by attention to experience and memory.

> **Wisdom is the daughter of experience.** – Leonardo da Vinci

> **Memory is the mother of all wisdom.** – Aeschylus

In addition, the wise person is open-minded, acknowledging their limitations with a cheerful willingness to learn more.

> **The cleverest of all, in my opinion, is the man who calls himself a fool at least once a month.** – Dostoevsky

Phronesis bestows both an understanding of first principles of general knowledge and good judgement, and a shrewd ability to apply what's appropriate to each situation. It involves being good at reasoning, evaluating evidence, and comparing alternatives.

Cicero translated the term as *providentia*, meaning foresight. The medieval Latin schoolmen contracted this into *prudentia*, referring to the ability to appreciate the uniqueness and complexity of any given situation, with appropriate awareness of the long-term risks and implications of each possible action.

Prudence. A woman puts out a fire before it spreads; a sick man is attended to; a merchant saves his gold; winter supplies are prepared and stored; the house is repaired. Engraved by Philips Galle [1537–1612] from an original drawing by Pieter Bruegel the Elder [1525–1569], Netherlands.

We have all met people lacking in prudence; they are shortsighted, thoughtless, distracted, negligent, and wasteful. Others twist their wisdom and become fraudulent, cunning, slick, sneaky, or deceitful.

Just as a masterful athlete or musician knows almost by feeling what's appropriate in a given context, so the *phronimos* knows how to make emotion an ally of reason. Such a person can rely on their well-formed passions to shape good judgment, especially in contexts where timing matters and a quick decision is needed.

> **Wisdom is better than rubies; and all the things that may be desired are not to be compared to it.** – Proverbs [8:11]

The Seven Deadly Sins
excess, inadequacy, and perversion

Dante Aligheri [1265–1321], in the *Divine Comedy*, has Virgil accompany him and his reader on a journey across seven terraces to diagnose and heal a broken soul. Dante argues that every virtue, as well as every vice, springs from love. Understood this way, sin is love that has wandered off the path; it is possible to love in a friendly and appropriate way, or in distorted ways. Dante's journey moves from the least serious disorders to the most serious. The easiest way to misdirect love is to place too much value on an earthly good, such as sexual pleasure (*lust*), food (*gluttony*), or possessions (*greed*). A less common, but more deadly, way to go astray is to lose interest in these, or in anything or anyone (*sloth*).

   With regard to the destruction of one's character, it is even more deadly to practice a distorted defiant love that takes perverse delight in the downfall of others. This can be done in three (progressively disordered) ways: desiring revenge (*wrath*), taking jealous delight in the possessions of another (*envy*), or exalting oneself above all others (*pride*). Of the seven, the most deadly is pride or vainglory, which Dante defined as "love of self perverted to hatred and contempt for one's neighbor."

LATIN	VICE	MISDIRECTED LOVE	OPPOSING VIRTUE
luxuria	LUST	*excessive love of sex*	courtly love
gula	GLUTTONY	*excessive love of food*	temperance
avaritia	GREED	*excessive love of material possessions*	generosity
acedia	SLOTH	*inadequate love of beginning anything*	zeal
ira	WRATH	*perverted love of revenge*	patience
invidia	ENVY	*perverted love of another's goods*	kindness
superbia	PRIDE	*perverted love of oneself*	humility

Dante drew from several lists of vices and virtues. One such seven-part list joined the four cardinal virtues (*p. 20*) with the three theological virtues: faith, hope, and charity. Gregory the Great [540–604] proposed another list of seven virtues that directly oppose the seven deadly sins, with humility at the root (*shown above*).

As to the Seven Deadly Sins, I deplore Pride, Wrath, Lust, Envy, and Greed. Gluttony and Sloth I pretty much plan my day around. – Robert Brault

Facing page: The Seven Deadly Sins, Dietrich Meyer [1572–1658]. Superbia gazes at herself in a mirror beside a peacock, Avaritia clutches her treasure in front of a toad, Invidia bites her nails while snakes writhe in her hair and an angry dog yaps at her heels, Ira strides forth armed with a sword and lion, Libido stands in for Luxuria, Ebrietas (intoxication) for Gluttony, and Otium (idleness) for Sloth.

Left: Triumph of Virtue over the Seven Deadly Sins, Venice, 1508. The sins are represented by animals, a goat for lust, a pig for gluttony, a toad for greed, an ass for sloth, a lion for wrath, a dog for envy, and a peacock for pride.

HUMILITY AND GREATNESS
a sense of perspective

St. Gregory the Great insisted that humility is a key virtue, and this has never been more true than today. Many aspects of modern societies positively encourage an inflated sense of one's own importance, and an unreflective belief that it is perfectly legitimate to expect and pursue the satisfaction of one's every desire.

> *Observe what has happened to the seven deadly sins of Christian theology. All but one of these sins, sloth, was transformed into a positive virtue. Greed, avarice, envy, gluttony, luxury and pride are the driving forces of the new economy.* – Lewis Mumford

The resulting lack of humility distorts relationships not only between people, but also between human beings and the rest of the world (*see pp. 52–55*). Like other virtues, humility is a mean condition between vices of excess and deficiency. So, avoiding pride, conceit, and *hubris*, the vices of excess, does not mean retreating into exaggerated self-abasement, or hiding one's light under a bushel. It means developing a properly balanced sense of one's true importance in the world.

This is an area where classical priorities can be at odds with those of today. Every culture touched by Homer is taught, in one way or another, to admire a trait Aristotle called *megalopsychia*, "greatness of soul." Magnanimous individuals such as Odysseus conduct themselves with an almost preternatural awareness of their own excellence and carry themselves with a sense of grandeur. When Aristotle describes *megalopsychoi* he praises the grand elder who walks slowly, speaks in a deep voice, and carries himself with a sense of his own *gravitas*.

But he also commends the ironist who, while aware of his status and accomplishments, knowingly presents himself with understated grace. Even in Athens, the proud swagger of the hero sometimes clashed with the gentle virtues of sophisticated society.

A virtuous person treats others respectfully, but without denying his or her own true worth. What does this mean in practice? Nowadays, we perhaps see humility as requiring us to treat others as equals, rather than in terms of respecting hierarchical power relations, as was often the case in former times. Questions about appropriate self-awareness and self-presentation still arise though, and are still important. Thinking them through can lead to the insight that being grounded and authentically humble is entirely compatible with greatness of soul. A great soul is, after all, also a humble one.

> *Humility, far from being opposed to magnanimity, serves to temper it, because humility makes us recognize great gifts.* – Pope Francis

> *It's better to be looked over than overlooked.* – Mae West

Pride leads her forces. From the celebrated Hortus Delicarum, *Hohenburg Abbey, Alsace, 1185, the first encyclopedia to be written by a woman.*

SOCIAL VIRTUES
gentleness, honesty, friendliness, and wit

Following Aristotle, Thomas Aquinas [c. 1225–1274] described the social virtues as those required in order to "behave well in the conduct of human affairs."

GENTLENESS: Gentleness defines the mean between excessive irascibility on the one hand and a lack of spirit on the other. A hot-headed person can quickly over-react to a perceived slight, while a bitter person can bottle it up until it explodes. The gentle person, with well ordered passions, finds the mean. Such a person gets angry about the right things, with the right people, in the right ways, at the right times.

Charity, cast out of the world by Self Interest (who has cut off her feet), is aided by a gentle and friendly poet. Peter Flötner, Nuremberg, early 1500s.

TRUTHFULNESS: We all prefer people who speak and act with integrity. Moreover, no society can function for long if people don't tell the truth, while expecting others to do so. Two stock characters from the ancient Greek stage typify excess and deficiency of this virtue: the *alazon* is a boaster who pretends to be greater than he is, and the *eiron* is a self-deprecator. Together, these two produce a humorous effect: the chubby bragger who overstates the truth is brought down a peg by the skinny, understated ironist. Their comic *hamartia* (missing-the-mark) brings into focus the target of truthfulness.

FRIENDLINESS: Friendliness is the disposition to treat strangers as future friends. Whether one's natural temperament is extraverted or introverted, one can develop an appropriate level of friendliness. A deficiency of friendliness results in a quarrelsome, contentious, cantankerous crank. An excess produces the annoyingly friendly, flattering, fawning, obsequious sycophant.

> *There's not a word yet for old friends who've just met.* – Bob Marley

WIT: Our contemporaries might not think much about the ethics of having a good sense of humor, but the ancients offer timeless insight into this aspect of the art of character:

> *Those who carry humor to excess are vulgar buffoons, pursuing what's funny at all costs, and doing anything to get a laugh without concern for the pain caused to those who are the butt of their jibes; while those who can neither make a joke themselves nor appreciate good humor are boorish and stiff. The one who jokes tastefully is witty and quick.* – Aristotle [1128a5]

> *You can pretend to be serious. You can't pretend to be witty.* – Sacha Guitry

FRIENDSHIP
sharing the good life

Ancient philosophers reflected deeply on the nature of friendship and its place in a good life, for it is crucial to the rhetorical practice of citizen leadership, and indispensable to human flourishing.

Of all possessions a friend is the most precious. – Herodotus

In classical antiquity, politicians and rhetoricians addressed fellow citizens as "friends." Thus, Mark Antony begins his funeral oration:

Friends, Romans, countrymen, lend me your ears. – Shakespeare, *Julius Caesar*

Friendship is the central topic of Plato's *Lysis*, while Aristotle devotes more space to *philia* than to any of the virtues, defining it as reciprocated goodwill (*eunoia*, "good minded") with mutual awareness. He says that the proper objects of love are what is *useful* or *pleasant* or *good* in itself:

Friendship takes three forms, equal in number to the proper objects of love. – [1156a6]

- A **FRIENDSHIP OF UTILITY** is characterized by reciprocated goodwill where each party is useful to each other: examples include business partnerships, relationships among co-workers, and study partners.

- A **FRIENDSHIP OF PLEASURE** centers on the delight that accompanies shared activity: a tennis partner or a theater-going companion.

These are both *coincidental friendships*: the love is related to how useful or pleasant the other is, and last only as long as the utility or pleasure.

A **COMPLETE FRIENDSHIP** is between good people who are alike in virtue. Each is attracted to the other's excellence, desiring what's best for the sake of the friend's well being. Such friendships endure, since virtue persists, but are rare, since they develop over time, are tested through shared difficulty, and require sustained closeness.

Cicero translates *eunoia* as *benevolentia*, the idea that friends relate to one another with shared concern, wanting what's good for each other. In his dialogue *Laelius de Amicitia* he explores the nature of friendship by puzzling through questions such as "how far should a friend go to aid a friend?" and "should new friends ever be put before old friends?" He emphasizes the importance of trust, frankness, equality, graciousness, and kindness between friends.

What sweetness is left in life, if you take away friendship? Robbing life of friendship is like robbing the world of the sun. – Cicero

Renaissance essayists such as Michel de Montaigne [1533–92] and Francis Bacon [1561–1626] also praised friendship in their writings.

Left: Illustration from The Paris Sketch Book of Mr M. A. Titmarsh, *by William Makepeace Thackeray [1811–63]. Does this look like a Friendship of Utility? of Pleasure? or a Complete Friendship?*

Friendships build bridges between sexes, tribes, classes, and ages. Like Cicero, today we still question friendship: Do happy people need friends? What is a workplace friend? Can citizen friendships affect large, modern nation-states? Can an internet friend be a genuine companion? Can a favorite author be a friend?

Good Society
sphaera civitatis

A Spartan herald is recorded as once having said to the Persian king:

> *You understand a slave's life, but, having never tasted freedom, you do not know the sweetness of liberty.* – Herodotus [484–425 BC]

Athenian democracy was, ironically, built on slavery. But for those who were granted it, citizenship in the *polis* entailed sharing political power. A citizen was neither a slave nor a subject, but was *sui juris*, able to manage their own affairs. They enjoyed the abundance of civilized life and took part in the governance of the community's pursuit of shared goods. So the practice of citizenship, then as now, contained an internal motive to become informed and engaged, to cultivate eloquence, participate in public debate, and exercise the moral and intellectual virtues requisite for social life amongst a self-governing people.

> *All that is valuable in human society depends upon the opportunity for development accorded the individual.* – Albert Einstein [1879–1955]

What sort of education is required for civic virtue? Beyond the technical expertise needed to be a productive member of society, citizens require *artes liberales*: the skills worthy of a free person that perfect language, thought, and character.

> *Freedom is absolutely necessary for progress in science and the liberal arts.*
> – Baruch Spinoza [1632–1677]

The scope and degrees of citizenship have generated centuries-long debates. In ancient Rome, *civitas*, the political space constructed by a people to live a distinctively human life, extended beyond urban boundaries to include *res publica*, "public things," of all kinds (this many-layered phrase is the root of the English word "republic").

Diogenes of Sinope [412–323 BC] proclaimed "I am a citizen of the world." Augustine of Hippo [354–430 AD] later extended this to dual citizenship, encouraging peaceful contribution to the earthly political community while participating as pilgrims of the heavenly city.

Today, "global citizenship," emphasizing the solidarity across political boundaries required to address global problems, contends with "localism," which prizes connection to place and maximal local participation in shared decision-making. In addressing this modern dilemma, as much as for the timeless task of shoring up civic life against corruption, the classic virtues remain indispensable.

A constitutional democracy is in serious trouble if its citizenry does not have a certain degree of education and civic virtue. – Philip Johnson

Left: Title page of John Case's Sphaera Civitatis, *a popular Aristotelian treatise on politics, first published in 1588. "Elizabeth, Queen of the Angles, the French and the Spanish, defender of the faith," presides over the Ptolemaic universe. Inside the celestial sphere, with its stars, nobles, heroes, and counselors, the planets rule the moral traits of good government: thus Majesty is ruled by Saturn, Prudence occupies the sphere of Jupiter, Fortitude is governed by Mars, Religion is the domain of the Sun, Mercury belongs to Venus, Eloquence to Mercy, and Abundance is the province of the Moon. At the center is "Immovable Justice."*

NATURAL LAW
a compass within

Is there is an innate moral law which guides human action? Plato and Aristotle hint at the idea, and Sophocles [497–405 BC] captures it in a speech delivered by Antigone to Creon:

> These laws are not for now or for yesterday. They are alive forever, and no one knows when they were first shown to us. – Sophocles, *Antigone*

Cicero later provided the classic Stoic expression of natural law philosophy when he argued that Tarquin's rape of Lucretia was illicit, regardless of human legislation:

> Although there was no written law concerning adultery during the reign of Tarquin, it does not therefore follow that Sextus Tarquinius did not offend against the eternal law when he committed a rape on Lucretia. For, even then he had the light of reason from the nature of things, that incites to good actions and dissuades from evil ones; and which does not begin for the first time to be a law when it is drawn up in writing. – Cicero, *de Legibus*

The apostle Paul wrote in his *Letter to the Romans* that every human has a conscience, "a law written on the heart," and during the high middle ages, Jewish, Christian, and Muslim scholars, from Baghdad to Cordova, interacted in tolerant harmony while debating the obligations of this natural law binding upon all.

One famous twentieth-century appeal to the idea of an objective norm for human conduct appears in the letter written by Martin Luther King, Jr. while imprisoned for protesting segregation laws:

How does one determine whether a law is just or unjust? A just law is a man made code that squares with the moral law or the law of God. An unjust law is a code that is out of harmony with the moral law. To put it in the terms of St. Thomas Aquinas: An unjust law is a human law that is not rooted in eternal law and natural law. Any law that uplifts human personality is just. Any law that degrades human personality is unjust. All segregation statutes are unjust because segregation distorts the soul and damages the personality. It gives the segregator a false sense of superiority and the segregated a false sense of inferiority. – Martin Luther King, Jr.

Human laws can certainly be just or unjust, and King was surely right that this is connected with whether a law uplifts or degrades those governed by it. Yet such insights alone cannot establish that any law is really "natural." The segregationists also thought their beliefs reflected natural law, as indeed did Aristotle when he claimed that some people were born to be slaves. Every society has those who claim that its own laws and culture reflect "how things ought to be." Subcultures and resistance movements do the same.

Timeless questions of what it is for a human being to flourish, and to treat others well, must be contemplated afresh by every generation.

The greatest good for a human is daily to converse about virtue. – Socrates

In the modern era, this search for an ethic that transcends culture and context has given us the idea of universal human rights.

HUMAN RIGHTS
universal values

John Locke argued in 1688 that the sole justification of government was to protect individuals' "natural rights" to life, liberty, and property. He saw such rights as deriving from principles of natural law, which in turn could be discovered by discerning the will of God. This established the important principle that individual rights could transcend the authority of the state, but left it open for disputes over "what God intended" to affect what rights people would have.

Immanuel Kant [1724–1804] later argued (*see p. 43*) that the claim that humans have certain fundamental rights could in fact be justified without appeal to any religious tradition. This cleared the way for modern universal human rights, but it would be another 200 years before they emerged into law.

In an effort to avoid any recurrence of the horrors of World War II, the Universal Declaration of Human Rights (UDHR) was adopted by the UN General Assembly in 1948 (*see the 30 articles, opposite*). For the first time, fundamental moral principles governing how we should treat one another were finally agreed to cover all human beings, as inalienable rights rather than as privileges of status or citizenship.

Since 1948 many other treaties and covenants on human rights have come into force, and the UDHR itself has gained the status of international law, meaning that every country's laws are supposed to be consistent with it. A moral right is not the same as a legal right, however, and the process of turning human rights from the former into the latter is far from complete.

Plato and Aristotle would have agreed that human affairs should be governed by universal moral principles, though their own cultural assumptions might have led them to disgree with many modern rights. Reaching agreement across cultures is hard, and debate continues, both about proposed new human rights and about some existing ones.

THE 30 ARTICLES OF THE UNIVERSAL DECLARATION OF HUMAN RIGHTS

1. Right to Equality
2. Freedom from Discrimination
3. Right to Life, Liberty, and Personal Security
4. Freedom from Slavery
5. Freedom from Torture and Degrading Treatment
6. Right to Recognition as a Person before the Law
7. Right to Equality before the Law
8. Right to Remedy by Competent Tribunal
9. Freedom from Arbitrary Arrest and Exile
10. Right to Fair Public Hearing
11. Right to be Considered Innocent until Proven Guilty
12. Freedom from Interference with Privacy, Family, Home & Correspondence
13. Right to Free Movement in and out of the Country
14. Right to Asylum in other Countries from Persecution
15. Right to a Nationality and the Freedom to Change It
16. Right to Marriage and Family
17. Right to Own Property
18. Freedom of Belief and Religion
19. Freedom of Opinion and Information
20. Right of Peaceful Assembly and Association
21. Right to Participate in Government and in Free Elections
22. Right to Social Security
23. Right to Desirable Work and to Join Trade Unions
24. Right to Rest and Leisure
25. Right to Adequate Living Standard
26. Right to Education
27. Right to Participate in the Cultural Life of Community
28. Right to a Social Order that Articulates this Document
29. Community Duties Essential to Free and Full Development
30. Freedom from State or Personal Interference in the above Rights.

THE GOLDEN RULE
do as you would be done by

The directive maxim Treat others as you would like them to treat you has been dubbed the "golden rule" at least since the 17th century, although versions can be found in the ancient codes of Egypt and Babylon, and in almost every world religion and wisdom tradition:

> *Regard your neighbor's gain as your own gain and your neighbor's loss as your own loss.* – Laozi, *Dao de jing*

> *Therefore all things whatsoever ye would that men should do to you, do ye even so to them.* – Bible, Matthew 7:12

> *No one of you is a believer until he desires for his brother that which he desires for himself.* – Sayings of Muhammad, Hadith 13

A prohibitive version, Do not treat others in ways you would not like to be treated, sometimes called the "silver rule," may be older:

> *Hurt not others in ways that you yourself would find hurtful.* – Udana-Varga 5:18

> *One should not behave towards others in a way which is disagreeable to oneself.*
> – Mahabharata, Anusasana Parva 113.8.

> *That which is hateful to you, do not do to your fellow. That is the whole Torah. The rest is elaboration. Go and learn.* – Torah, Shabbath 31a

DO UNTO OTHERS AS YOU WOULD HAVE THEM DO TO YOU.

But what if you're a masochist...?

DUTY
a little respect

Immanuel Kant argued that the Golden Rule need not be taken on scriptural authority, since it followed logically from a moral duty of *respect for persons*:

> *Act in such a way as to treat humanity, whether in your own person or in that of anyone else, always as an end and never merely as a means.* – Kant

> *Do your duty as you see it, and damn the consequences.* – George S. Patton

Deontology (from the Greek *deon*, duty) is the name for moral theories, like Kant's, which claim that certain actions are right or wrong in themselves, regardless of the consequences that may follow. Because he believed the "moral law" prescribed what one should do in all cases, Kant called it a *categorical imperative*. One expression of this, the *principle of universalizability*, asks whether the maxim guiding a proposed course of action is one that everyone should adopt:

> *Act only according to that maxim by which you can at the same time will that it should become a universal law for all humankind.* – Kant

A quick test, leading straight back to the Golden Rule, is the principle of reversibility: "Would I want my proposed action done to me?"

Telling lies, for instance, treats others as a means to one's own ends. It is also not something anyone could realistically wish everyone to do, so it violates both versions of the categorical imperative. However:

> DILEMMA: *What if a raging man wielding an axe asks you which way his intended victim went? Would it really be wrong to lie?*

43

UTILITY AND EQUALITY
consequences for all

Deontology holds that some actions, such as murder, are always wrong, no matter what. *Utilitarianism*, by contrast, is interested solely in outcomes. For a utilitarian, the end can justify the means: so perhaps killing one person to save ten might be right?

> DILEMMA: *A villain holds you and ten other people hostage, and then orders you to murder one of your fellow prisoners. You are told that if you do not do the murder then all ten of the others will be executed. What should you do?*

Jeremy Bentham [1748–1832], who coined the term utilitarianism, wanted ethics to be based solely on evidence, in the form of measurable consequences. Ethics was simply a matter of "summing up all the values of pleasure on one side, and those of all the pains on the other," thereby calculating the net impact on human happiness of any proposed action.

It is the greatest happiness of the greatest number that is the measure of right and wrong. – Jeremy Bentham [1776]

The hostage dilemma (*above*) illustrates some of the attractions of utilitarianism, but also some of its shortcomings. Not even Jeremy Bentham would really feel happy about killing his fellow prisoner. Just as with deontology's formal principles of duty, utilitarianism's

"It's a government funded study to find out how many wrongs make a right."

44

bald calculations often seem to miss something important.

Bentham saw utilitarianism as an emancipatory project, which could make society fairer and more equal. He wanted the pleasures and pains of *everyone* to be counted and measured on a single scale, not just those of men, of the rich and privileged, or of the well-educated. He felt it was the happiness that mattered, not how it was produced.

"Do you realize what Ethics has cost us this year?"

> *Prejudice apart, the game of push-pin is of equal value with the arts and sciences of music and poetry.* – Jeremy Bentham [c. 1775]

John Stuart Mill [1826–1873] later developed his own version of utilitarianism, which argued that "higher" pleasures such as poetry should be seen as better than "lower" pleasures such as push-pin (a popular bar game of the time).

> *It is better to be a human being dissatisfied than a pig satisfied; better to be Socrates dissatisfied than a fool satisfied.* – John Stuart Mill [1863]

Of course, while this version works well for poetry enthusiasts, it doesn't look so good if you prefer the joys of push-pin. Nobody wants to be seen as the pig. Is this just elitism, or an argument for good education and public subsidy of the arts? This debate continues today, in parliaments as well as universities.

ETHICS IN REAL LIFE
calculation or judgment?

A great deal of what passes for ethical deliberation these days is essentially utilitarianism. Whether a proposed action or policy would be right or wrong is widely seen to depend entirely on whether it will have a desirable outcome, all things considered. Since it's so hard to "sum up" all the different pleasures and pains felt by everyone affected by a given action or decision, such calculations often try and translate these into financial values, the better to add and subtract them.

> DILEMMA: *The time saved for thousands of commuting drivers by widening a congested urban highway is valued at more than the compensation owed to those whose houses will be demolished. Should the road be widened?*

But even if it were possible to put a price on everything, would it be right? Ethics is not just an exercise in cost-benefit analysis.

Ethical dilemmas can be approached several ways. A utilitarian perspective measures the *outcome*, a deontological perspective focuses on the *act*, and a virtue perspective considers the *character* of the agent:

> DILEMMA: *A runaway train is heading downhill towards five people working on the line. You can divert the train onto a disused siding where you know one homeless man is asleep on the tracks. What should you do?*

A pure Kantian would probably not divert the train, since this would deliberately kill an innocent person, an act which is always wrong. A pure utilitarian would probably be prepared to kill one innocent person in order to save five. A virtue ethicist would begin by applying practical wisdom in order to discern what other virtues

"THAT'S IT, IN A NUTSHELL."

(such as courage and justice) might be appropriate to this unfortunate situation, and then consider how to act in such a way as to embody them (requiring more detail than is specified here).

Virtue ethics is thus not well suited to giving quick answers to lurid hypothetical dilemmas such as these, which are designed to expose differences between "right" as valued by deontologists, and "good" as valued by utilitarians. They present a clear choice whether or not to do something that appears wrong, in order to avert an apparently greater evil. Real life ethical decisions tend to be less clear-cut, and more complicated. Many ethicists today seek to integrate useful aspects of modern moral theories with a renewed focus on virtue.

When determining moral responsibility, many ethicists also distinguish between a person's intention and foreseeable side effects. So, physicians sometimes prescribe palliative sedation to relieve suffering at the end of life, foreseeing unintended effects, including the death of a patient, and in military ethics, a tactical weapon, aimed at military target, may have the foreseen side effect of inciting fear and causing civilian deaths. Is foreseeing an outcome morally different than intending it?

DEPENDENCE
and caring for others

Many of the trickiest ethical decisions arise when not all the people involved are equal, healthy, rational adults.

> DILEMMA: *Your five-year-old daughter is too sick for school, but you have arranged to visit your aged father today. He lives alone, cannot hear the phone, and will become very anxious if you don't turn up. What should you do?*

Human flourishing involves self-governance and resilience, while justice requires us to respect the dignity and self-direction of others. But we do not come into this world as independent practical reasoners. If we achieve flourishing in this life, we do so only after long periods of dependence, relying on the generous care of others, whether in childhood, illness, disability, or old age. As Alasdair MacIntyre notes, English has no equivalent to the Lakota Sioux term *wancantognaka*, the virtue of open-hearted recognition of reliance on others.

Some feminist writers on *relational ethics* upend Plato's ordering of the Republic over the family, suggesting that ethics in fact has its origin in the home, especially in parental love. Building an understanding of ethics outwards from such relationships of care can throw a very different light on larger scale issues of social policy.

"I made this Valentine's card for you in school, mom. What the world needs is more love, and less homework."

48

MEDICAL ETHICS
first, do no harm

Utilitarian reasoning is not as dominant in medicine as elsewhere, partly because medical ethics has an ancient pedigree. This dates at least to the Oath written by Hippocrates (or one of his followers) between the 5th and 3rd century BC, in which physicians vow to comport themselves in a godly manner and never misuse their position.

Modern medical ethics proposes four action-guiding principles:

NON-MALEFICENCE: *Often expressed more pithily as "First, do no harm."*

BENEFICENCE: *The practitioner must act in the best interest of the patient.*

RESPECT FOR AUTONOMY: *The patient has the right to choose or refuse treatment. This includes the sub-principle of* INFORMED CONSENT: *the patient must be given all the information required for such decisions.*

JUSTICE: *Who gets what treatment should be decided fairly and equitably.*

It is not only possible but common for two or more of these principles to come into conflict, giving rise to complex ethical dilemmas:

DILEMMA: *A critically injured road accident victim refuses a blood transfusion, citing her beliefs as a Jehovah's Witness. Her relatives say she converted only recently, under pressure from a manipulative new boyfriend. Should doctors perform the transfusion?*

DILEMMA: *Two patients need a new kidney equally urgently, but only one is available. Which patient should get it?*

Difficult decisions like these are made by doctors every day.

ETHICS AT WORK
roles and responsibilities

In the case of doctors, ethics is clearly important. But ethical considerations apply whatever we do for a living. While we're used to hearing about "ethical consumerism," taking ethics to work with us is at least as important as taking them to the supermarket.

Sometimes the right course of action is obvious, and reflected in the rules of the job. Teachers shouldn't accept favors from students (or their parents) in exchange for better grades. Train drivers shouldn't drink on duty. Building inspectors shouldn't accept bribes to sign off unsafe structures. However, other cases are trickier:

> SCENARIO: *A man is struggling to meet the costs of caring for his disabled child. He secretly takes home some out-of-date food from the grocery store where he works, against company rules. Is this wrong?*

> DILEMMA: *A policewoman has a close cousin who is a single parent and occasional drug user. Should she tip her off about a forthcoming drug raid?*

People holding public office or managing public resources have clear responsibilities not to abuse their position. But private businesses run for profit also wield great power and can often do things which, while legal, may seem unethical.

SCENARIO: *A car company buys up local bus companies and shuts them down, increasing demand for its own products. Surely this is just business?*

SCENARIO: *A global water company buys the water supply infrastructure of a poor city and raises the price of water tenfold, making it unaffordable for many.*

Such matters are sometimes addressed by corporate social responsibility (CSR) policies, with varying degrees of effectiveness. But what happens if these kinds of unethical practices are intrinsic to the core business of the company and returns for its shareholders?

SCENARIO: *A pharmaceutical company specializes in buying up patents on old drugs still in widespread use, then raising the prices.*

Ethics are relevant to all employees, not just management, and the need to earn a living doesn't justify unethical behavior. Conversely no one should have to do things at work they wouldn't be prepared to do as a private individual, including turning a blind eye to wrongdoing:

DILEMMA: *Anna, an insurance saleswoman, discovers her colleague Barry is misleading elderly clients into buying expensive policies they don't need. She tells her boss, but he says she'll be sacked if she mentions it again, so she pretends not to know. Who's in the wrong?*

Many countries have "whistleblower protection" laws to protect individuals who come forward in just these kinds of situation.

ETHICS AND ANIMALS
reaching out beyond the human

Most of ethics has always been about how to treat our fellow humans, and being human has often been defined by contrast with "beasts" or "dumb animals." Yet concern for animal suffering has a long history. The philosopher and mathematician Pythagoras [c. 580–500 BC] was a vegetarian, apparently for ethical as well as health reasons:

> *As long as man continues to be the ruthless destroyer of lower living beings he will never know health or peace. For as long as men massacre animals, they will kill each other. Indeed, he who sows the seed of murder and pain cannot reap joy and love.* – Pythagoras [attributed by Ovid]

This kind of virtue-based argument, still common today, claims that someone who treats animals badly debases their character, and so will treat people badly too. Some utilitarians, such as Peter Singer [1946–], agree with Jeremy Bentham (*see p. 44*) that the pleasures and pains of animals should also be taken into account:

> *The question is not, can they reason? Nor can they talk? But, can they suffer?*
> – Jeremy Bentham [1780]

Mostly though, modern utilitarian reasoning has not been good for animals. Farming animals for food perhaps need not involve suffering, though most modern versions do:

> DILEMMA: *Over 50 billion chickens are killed and eaten worldwide by humans every year. Most have been kept in close confinement and actively prevented from having a normal chicken's life. Is this acceptable?*

Vivisection is another related matter:

DILEMMA: *Millions of animals suffer and die every year in the safety testing of chemicals, drugs, and consumer products. Is this justifiable?*

Both utilitarians like Singer and some Kantians (such as Tom Regan), have supported greater respect for animals on *extensionist* grounds. They argue that over the last 2500 years the circle of moral considerability has expanded from Athenian men to include women, the poor, and other ethnic groups: should this expansion not continue to include at least some animals? Exactly what this would mean, and which animals should be included, raises many questions, but most extensionists would start with those most similar to us:

DILEMMA: *Chimpanzees share 99% of their DNA with humans. Orangutans and gorillas face extinction. Should we extend basic legal rights (to life, liberty, and freedom from torture) to our closest cousins, the other great apes?*

Environmental Ethics
care for our common home

If applying traditional ethics to animals is difficult, then applying them to environmental problems is harder still. Yet there is clearly a strong ethical dimension to the current crisis in human relationships with the nonhuman world. Ethicists have puzzled over how to accommodate inspiring insights such as those expressed by Aldo Leopold:

> *A thing is right when it tends to preserve the integrity, stability, and beauty of the biotic community. It is wrong when it tends otherwise.* – A Sand County Almanac

One way of doing so is by way of ethical extensionism (*see p. 52*). Perhaps animals, plants, even landscapes and ecosystems, are due respect in their own right and (as Kant said about people) should never be treated merely as means to human ends.

DILEMMA: *Across the world, trees are threatened by development. To facilitate their protection, should trees have legal standing in court, enabling lawyers to argue directly for their interests? If corporations and states can be treated as legal persons, why not the natural environment?*

"WE BELIEVE WE WILL BE ABLE TO TEAR DOWN THE ENTIRE ECOSYSTEM IN AN ENVIRONMENTALLY FRIENDLY MANNER."

This suggestion, made by Christopher Stone in 1972, might seem fanciful, but reflecting indigenous belief systems, the constitutions of Ecuador and Bolivia do now explicitly recognize rights for nature (or "*Pachamama*").

Another approach is to consider the interests of future humans:

DILEMMA: *What do our obligations to future generations require us to bequeath them?*

It's hard to know exactly what future people will value. But that's no reason not to leave them a natural world at least as wonderful as the one we enjoy today. If we take this obligation seriously, there's plenty of work to be done.

Environmental virtue ethics takes a different approach again, asking as usual what virtues are relevant to the problem, and what it would mean to embody them. Humility seems key (*see p. 32*), as does moderation (*p. 25*), and wisdom and courage will certainly be required. Some argue that it may be helpful to think in terms of a new virtue such as what Rosalind Hursthouse calls "right orientation to nature."

A virtue approach makes clear that working for ecological sustainability is not a matter of sacrificing the present for the sake of the future. Practicing ecological virtue and good stewardship contributes to human flourishing for everyone, right now.

LEARNING AND LIVING
ars recte vivendi

The liberal arts are traditionally divided into the *trivium* (three paths), involving the proper exercise of language (grammar, logic, and rhetoric) and the *quadrivium* (four paths), concerning number (arithmetic, music, geometry, and astronomy). Unlike the content-based *quadrivium*, the *trivium* are preliminary disciplines which are methods for dealing with subjects, roads that lead the lively mind to "learn how to learn," and quest for wisdom hidden in the "art of character" and the "art of living."

> To compose our character is our duty, not to compose books, and to win, not battles and provinces, but order and tranquility in our conduct. Our great and glorious masterpiece is to live appropriately. All other things, ruling, hoarding, building, are only little appendages and props, at most. – Michel de Montaigne [1533 – 1592]

Choosing the right word for any context requires good judgment; learning grammar requires temperance and an appreciation for deep structures of human awareness; learning dialectical argumentation requires patience and focus; persuasive communication, when practiced artfully, leads to larger questions of human action and purpose.

We can puzzle about human actions from a range of perspectives. Looking back at past actions raises questions as to whether obligations were met; looking ahead to future actions invites consideration of the most beneficial plan or policy. But ethics is more than debating which action is right; it involves reflection on a whole life, and the fundamental issue of what makes for a good one.

Consider your deepest longings. Desire prompts action, and action in turn refines and consolidates character, thus shaping future desires. Accordingly, the human act of learning how to learn makes possible wise reflection and moral transformation.

Every human life is inevitably a self-portrait: the art of living is an art of character. Making a good and beautiful life thus requires crafting one's soul in excellence.

Above: The title page of the Margarita Philosophica (The Pearl of Wisdom), by Gregor Reisch [1467–1525], showing the Seven Liberal Arts as the leaves of the Tree of Knowledge.

APPENDIX - LIST OF VIRTUES

This list has been compiled from Hindu, Buddhist, Greek, Roman, Jewish, Christian, Islamic, and other sources. On the left of each virtue appears a vice corresponding to a deficiency of that virtue; on the right a vice of excess.

resistance **Acceptance** submissiveness
compliance **Assertiveness** aggression
insignificance **Authority** tyranny
ugliness **Beauty** gaudiness
animosity **Benevolence** downiness
neglectfulness **Caring** apprehensiveness
avarice **Charity** relinquishment
promiscuity **Chastity** frigidity
recklessness **Caution** timidity
dirtiness **Cleanliness** sterility
half-heartedness **Commitment** obsession
indifference **Compassion** sentimentality
self-doubt **Confidence** arrogance
selfishness **Consideration** selflessness
unhappiness **Contentment** complacency
divisiveness **Cooperation** dependence
cowardice **Courage** recklessness
rudeness **Courtesy** obeisance
unimaginativeness **Creativity** ungroundedness
disinterest **Curiosity** intrusiveness
submission **Defiance** unruliness
entanglement **Detachment** isolationism
irresolution **Determination** stubbornness
apathy **Devotion** infatuation
mindlessness **Diligence** laboriousness
stupidity **Discernment** fussiness
thoughtlessness **Discretion** vacillation
chaos **Discipline** unforgivingness
inarticulation **Eloquence** loquacity
self-obsession **Empathy** distress
indifference **Enthusiasm** mania
imbalance **Equanimity** dullness

inferiority **Excellence** perfectionism
skepticism **Faith** fundamentalism
prejudice **Fairness** indecision
rigidity **Flexibility** mutability
tangentiality **Focus** fixation
indulgence **Forbearance** abstinence
mercilessness **Forgiveness** indulgence
falseness **Frankness** insensitivity
hostility **Friendliness** overfamiliarity
lavishness **Frugality** meanness
meanness **Generosity** ostentatiousness
roughness **Gentleness** effeteness
godlessness **Grace** sanctimoniousness
unthankfulness **Gratitude** indebtedness
triviality **Gravitas** unapproachability
obstructiveness **Helpfulness** servility
deceitfulness **Honesty** naivete
humiliation **Honor** vainglory
despair **Hope** fantasy
callousness **Humanity** hypersensitivity
conceit **Humility** self-abasement
dullness **Humor** foolishness
unprincipledness **Integrity** overscrupulousness
biased **Impartiality** ineffectualness
laziness **Industry** frenzy
corruption **Innocence** vulnerability
misery **Joyfulness** idiocy
unfairness **Justice** prescriptiveness
cruelty **Kindness** indulgence
inability **Knowledge** dogmatism
fundamentalism **Liberality** permissiveness
coldness **Love** attachment
treachery **Loyalty** bondage
pitilessness **Mercy** leniency
indulgence **Moderation** self-denial
brazenness **Modesty** prudery
indiscipline **Obedience** slavishness
defensiveness **Openness** defenselessness

frustration **Patience** passivity
violence **Peacefulness** spinelessness
irresolution **Perseverance** protraction
godlessness **Piety** unction
stupidity **Prudence** calculation
lateness **Punctuality** chronocentrism
drift **Purposefulness** preoccupation
dissolute **Rectitude** inflexibility
inconstancy **Reliability** burden
remorselessness **Repentance** self-reproach
incapacity **Resourcefulness** expediency
irreverence **Respect** awe
contemptibility **Respectability** conventionality
immaturity **Responsibility** liability
self-indulgence **Restraint** suppression
disrespect **Reverence** deference
amorality **Righteousness** moralistic
solipsism **Service** vassalage
insensitivity **Sensitivity** rawness
brashness **Silence** shyness
overelaboration **Simplicity** vapidness
falsity **Sincerity** simplicity
drunkenness **Sobriety** temperance
inertia **Spontaneity** whimsy
fickleness **Steadfastness** inflexibility
weakness **Strength** brutality
yielding **Sternness** severity
indiscretion **Tact** fear
wastefulness **Thrift** austerity
prejudice **Tolerance** laxness
brittle **Toughness** stubbornness
suspiciousness **Trust** guilelessness
dishonor **Trustworthiness** unsuspecting
deceitfulness **Truthfulness** tactlessness
discord **Unity** uniformity
lifelessness **Vitality** mania
ignorance **Wisdom** bookish
certainty **Wonder** bewilderment
indifference **Zeal** fanaticism